_____'s

(your name here)

Prayers

Getting started...

Do you want to talk to God? Because He wants to hear you talk. He likes to hear about your day. He loves the chance to forgive you when you've done something wrong. He's happy when you thank Him. He's delighted when you tell Him how great He is. He's eager to help you when you need help and to help your friends when you tell Him they need help, too. He wants to hear what you're afraid of and what you're excited about. He smiles big when you tell Him how much You love Him.

God loves it when you talk to Him.
Sometimes we get a little scared when we think about talking to God. Maybe we don't know what to say to someone so important and powerful. Maybe we think we'll say something dumb or wrong. Maybe we just forget to talk to God. Or get too busy with homework and soccer practice and taking care of the cat.

The job of this journal is to help you talk to God. To give you ideas of what to say. To remind you of the kinds of things God wants to hear from you. It's also a way to make praying a habit, something you do every single day. When you talk to God every day, you and God get close. Isn't it amazing that you could be friends with God? You can! And this journal will help.

NUTS & BOLTS

Here's how the journal works: Each week you'll pray six prayers, one per day, Monday through Saturday. Every day you'll pray a different type of prayer. Here's a list of the six kinds of prayers you'll pray and why we pray each one:

Mondays: The Lord's Prayer
To begin our week, we'll pray like Jesus did. The book of Matthew is the story of Jesus living here on earth and was written by one of Jesus' best friends. In chapter 4, Jesus' followers ask Him how to pray. Jesus responds with the prayer we call "The Lord's Prayer." He says, "When you pray, pray like this." Every Monday we'll pray the way Jesus said we should.

Tuesdays: Praise
God is our King and Creator. He's big and important, and one of the most important things we do when we pray is to tell Him how great He is. That's what "praise" is--telling God how great He is. When you praise, you get the chance to think about how awesome God is and to remember the awesome things God's done. Praising God is a little like writing a love letter, because praise is where you tell God everything you like about Him.

Wednesdays: Connection

On Wednesdays we get the chance to talk to God like we talk to our parents or friends. These connection prayers will help you talk to God about all kinds of things--what you're nervous about, what you're interested in, how your day went, or why you like your favorite TV show so much. God likes you, and He wants to hear about the things you care about.

Thursdays: Thanksgiving

Just like you want to be thanked for the good things you do for other people, God wants to be thanked for the good things He does for you. And He does so many good things! The Bible tells us, "Every good action and every perfect gift is from God. These good gifts come down from the Creator of the sun, moon, and stars." When you're trying to thank God every day, you're more likely to see all the good things God's doing, and that makes you love God more. It makes you happier, too.

Fridays: Wants & Needs

You need stuff. You need help and courage and love. You need food and a home. You want stuff too. You want to feel better when you're sick. You want friends who'll be kind to you. You want a baby brother. God can help. He's powerful. He makes impossible things possible. He might not give you everything you ask for, but He loves the chance to give you what's good for you.

Saturdays: Intercession

Intercession is a fancy word that means praying for other

people. When we pray these prayers we'll be asking God to help and do good for the people in our families, churches, and schools. We'll also ask God to help people we've never met. When we have the chance to talk to the most important Person in the universe, we don't want to only talk about ourselves. We want to use our time with God to help others.

On Sundays we'll take a break. Probably on Sunday you'll get the chance to pray at church with your church family.

Those are the types of prayers we'll pray. You'll pray one a day, six days every week for thirteen weeks. Thirteen weeks equals one quarter of the year or one season. You might want to put the day's date at the top of your prayers.

One more thing: You're probably used to saying your prayers out loud or in your head. Because it's sometimes hard to concentrate when you say your prayers, this journal encourages you to write your prayers. Sometimes you'll even draw pictures. Don't worry about spelling your words the right way or using capital letters or putting periods on the ends of your sentences. God knows what you're writing, and He loves it.

Happy praying!

WEEK 1

Monday
//THE LORD'S PRAYER//

Today we'll pray The Lord's Prayer, the prayer Jesus taught His followers to pray. Read it first. Try to understand it. Then read the explanation. Finally, read it again, but this time say it to God.

Our Father Who is in Heaven,
Hallowed be Your name.
Your kingdom come, Your will be done
On earth as it is in Heaven.
Give us this day our daily bread
And forgive us our sins as we forgive those who sin against
us.
Lead us not into temptation but deliver us from the evil one.

Explanation:
The prayer starts with the words "Our Father." God is your dad, and you can talk to Him like He is!

Next we say "who is in Heaven." We pray to a God who lives up in Heaven, a kingdom we'll live in with Him one day.

"Hallowed be Your name" just means, "Special and honored be Your name." We pray that God would be recognized by every-one as different and better.

Next we ask God "Your kingdom come, Your will be done." We're asking God to do His good work here on earth, to make earth more like Heaven.

Then, we ask for "daily bread." That's asking God to give us what we need.

Next we ask God to forgive us for the things we've done wrong, and we promise God we'll forgive people who do wrong things to us.

Finally, we ask God to help us make good choices, to protect us from making bad choices and listening to the devil.

Tuesday
//PRAISE//

Describe God to God. Tell Him what He's like:

God, You are so...

_____

And

_____

And

_____

And

_____

Wednesday
//CONNECTION//

How was your day today? Tell God about it. Tell Him what you had for breakfast and who you talked to at school and how you did on your quiz. Tell Him everything...

Dear God,

_____

_____

_____

_____

_____

_____

_____

_____

_____

_____

_____

_____

_____

_____

_____

_____

_____

Thursday
//THANKS//

Every good gift is from God. What's good in your life right now? Make a list of good things:

1.

2.

3.

4.

5.

6.

7.

Now, say "Thank You, God, for..." each thing on your list, one by one.

Friday
//WANTS & NEEDS//

List three goals you have. Ask God to help you achieve them.

1.

2.

3.

You can also ask God to help you set good, beautiful goals that would make Him happy.

Saturday
//INTERCESSION//

Pray for your family members. List them here (or draw pictures of them):

What do you want God to do for them? How do you want God to help them? Ask Him.

WEEK 2

Monday
//The Lord's Prayer//

Today let's try to memorize The Lord's Prayer so you can say it wherever you are, whenever you need to say it. Copy the prayer two times using the space provided. Think about the words. Be sure to pay attention to what you're asking God.

Our Father Who is in Heaven,
Hallowed be Your name.
Your kingdom come, Your will be done
On earth as it is in Heaven.
Give us this day our daily bread
And forgive us our sins
as we forgive those who sin against us.
Lead us not into temptation
but deliver us from the evil one.

Tuesday
//PRAISE//

Sometimes we can best describe a thing by describing something else it's like. Today, compare God to things in order to understand (and praise) God better.

For example, you might pray, "God, You are like a battery. You give power." Or "God, You are like a tree. You're big and strong and beautiful."

Draw a picture on the next page to illustrate your comparisons.

God, You are like a _____.

You _____

_____.

God, You are like a _____.

You _____

_____.

Wednesday
//CONNECTION//

Have you ever felt embarrassed? What happened? Tell God all about it.

"Don't be embarrassed because you will not be disgraced. You will forget the shame you felt."
Isaiah 53:4

Thursday
//THANKSGIVING//

Pretend you're writing God a thank you note. Pick one or two gifts God's given you to thank Him for. You might tell Him how you've used the gifts or why you appreciate them so much.

Dear God,

Thank You so much for _____

_____

_____

_____

_____

_____

_____

_____

Love,

Friday
//WANTS & NEEDS//

In the book of Galatians the apostle Paul lists what he calls "the fruit of the Spirit." These "fruits" are gifts given to us by God, gifts that make us better people. Today, ask God to fill you with His Spirit and grow in you the fruit of His Spirit:

Dear God, Fill me with your Spirit. Give me the fruit of your Spirit:

Love

Joy

Peace

Patience

Kindness

Goodness

Faithfulness

Gentleness

&

Self Control

In Jesus' name I ask for You, God, to make me better, Amen.

Saturday
//INTERCESSION//

Name the kids in your class at school (write as many names below as you can remember). Pray for every girl and boy by name. Ask God to lead your classmates closer to Him. Pray specifically for friends who need help.

WEEK 3

Monday
//THE LORD'S PRAYER//

This week we'll use The Lord's Prayer as a skeleton. It'll be the bones of your prayer. Just answer the questions as you get to them...

Our Father who is in Heaven, hallowed be Your name. (How would you praise God? Write two words that describe how great He is.)

Your kingdom come, Your will be done, on earth as it is in Heaven. (Where do you see God's will NOT being done? Ask God to come there--maybe to a friend who doesn't love God, maybe to a family member who's not kind, maybe to your school... Write two people or places below.)

Give us this day our daily bread. (What do you need from God today?)

Forgive us our sins as we forgive those who sin against us. (Ask God to forgive you of things you've done wrong. Has anyone done something to hurt you? Tell God you're going to forgive them.)

Lead us not into temptation, but deliver us from the evil one. (Is the devil trying to convince you to do something bad? Tell God about it and ask for His help and protection.)

Tuesday
//PRAISE//

King David wrote this poem to praise God. Read it and praise
God alongside the giant-killing king. It's Psalm 145 in your Bible:

I praise Your greatness, my God the King.
I will praise You forever and ever.
I will praise You every day.
I will praise You forever and ever.
The Lord is great...

Parents will tell their children what you have done.
They will retell Your mighty acts,
wonderful majesty and glory...

They will remember Your great goodness.
They will sing about Your fairness.
The Lord is kind and shows mercy.
He does not become angry quickly but is full of love.
The Lord is good to everyone.

Wednesday
//CONNECTION//

Who do you want to be like when you grow up? What do you like about him or her? Tell God. Ask Him to help make you like that. (Either write your prayer below or draw a picture of the person you want to be like.)

Thursday
//THANKSGIVING//

Are you dealing with anything hard, confusing or frustrating?
In the middle of hard things it's helpful to look for God and the
good things He's doing. Try giving thanks even when things are
hard. If you get bullied at school, is there anyone who's nice you
can thank God for? If your parents are fighting, is there another adult in your life who's kind to you? Thank God for her. You
might also thank God for the hard thing itself. You might say,
"Thank You, God, for the kid at school who makes me fun of
me. I'm learning to forgive other people." Pick a hard thing and
pray.

Friday
//WANTS & NEEDS//

What have you done wrong lately? Are you feeling guilty for anything? Tell God about it and ask for forgiveness.

God, I'm sorry for...

Saturday
//INTERCESSION//

Pray for your leaders. Look up the names of the following national and local leaders. Fill in the blanks. Ask God to give these leaders wisdom, compassion, and courage. Ask God to help them use their power for good.

Your US President _____

Your state governor _____

Your city's mayor _____

Your school principal _____

Do you know any other leaders you'd like to pray for?

WEEK 4

Monday
//THE LORD'S PRAYER//

Today let's try saying The Lord's Prayer in your own words. Don't say it exactly how it's written. Instead try to say what the prayer means in words you understand better. Re-write each line in a new, easier way.

Our Father Who is in Heaven,
Hallowed be Your name.

Your kingdom come, Your will be done
On earth as it is in Heaven.

Give us this day our daily bread

And forgive us our sins as we forgive those who sin against us.

Lead us not into temptation but deliver us from the evil one.

Tuesday
//PRAISE//

Last week we read a poem from King David to God. Today, write your own poem telling God how great He is. Remember: Not all poems have to rhyme.

Wednesday
//CONNECTION//

What are you afraid of? Tell God all about it.

"Don't be afraid.
The Lord your God will be with you everywhere you go."
Joshua 1:9

Thursday
//THANKSGIVING//

Thank God for the Bible. Tell God two reasons you're glad to have the Bible.

1.

2.

Tell Him which story is your favorite. Draw it here:

Friday
//WANTS & NEEDS//

Do you need help with something? Write about it. Ask God for the help only He can give. Remember, God likes to help, and He's super good at giving it.

"Listen to my cry for help. My King and my God, I pray to You."
Psalm 5:2

Saturday
//INTERCESSION//

Do you have friends or relatives who're sick? Make a list of people you know who need healing. Ask God to make them better.

WEEK 5

Monday

//THE LORD'S PRAYER//

Have you memorized The Lord's Prayer yet? Try to recite it from memory.

Today, let's focus on the first line: "Our Father Who is in Heaven."

Tell God the ways He's a good Father. What does He do that a good father would do? How is He even better than the good fathers you know?

Tuesday
//PRAISE//

Make a list of amazing things God has done in the past. You can list things from the Bible or from your life. Read your list to God.

1.

2.

3.

4.

5.

Wednesday
//CONNECTION//

Do you have any friends or family members who're hard to get along with? Tell God about it. Tell Him what you're doing to try to get along with them.

"So let us try to do what makes peace and helps one another."
Romans 14:19

Thursday
//THANKSGIVING//

Make a list of your favorites (or draw them) below. Thank God for them:

Favorite food:

Favorite teacher:

Favorite subject in school:

Favorite book:

Favorite color:

Favorite animal:

Friday
//WANTS & NEEDS//

What do you want to get better at? How do you want to grow? What do you want to stop doing or start doing? Make a list of 5 areas for improvement. Then, ask God to help make you better in those areas.

1.

2.

3.

4.

5.

Saturday
//INTERCESSION//

Today, all over the world, Christians are being mistreated because they believe in Jesus. Here are a few of the most dangerous countries in the world for Christians. Pray for your brothers and sisters in these countries. Pray that they'd have courage to stand up for what they believe and that they'd have joy even when things are hard. You might also look up these countries on a map.

North Korea

Somalia

Iraq

Syria

Afghanistan

Sudan

Iran

Pakistan

WEEK 6

Monday
//THE LORD'S PRAYER//

Use The Lord's Prayer as a skeleton for your conversation with God. Remember: skeletons are the bones that hold something up.

Add your own words to The Lord's Prayer below:

Our Father Who is in Heaven, hallowed be Your name. (Add some praise here...)

Your kingdom come, Your will be done, on earth as it is in Heaven. (Ask God to do something good for people who don't know Him yet.)

Give us this day our daily bread. (What do you need from God?)

Forgive us our sins as we forgive those who sin against us. (This is where you confess your sins)

Lead us not into temptation, but deliver us from the evil one. (Ask God for any help you need in fighting the devil.)

Tuesday
//PRAISE//

Read this description of God in Numbers 23:18.
"God is not a man. He will not lie. God is not a human being.
He does not change his mind. What He says He will do, He
does. What He promises, He keeps."

Tell God what you learned about Him from this verse. Is this
good news about God? Why?

Wednesday
//CONNECTION//

If you and God were sitting down for lunch and you could ask Him anything, what would you ask Him? Why don't you go ahead and ask Him now? Ask God three questions. Write them below.

1.

2.

3.

Thursday
//THANKSGIVING//

Draw your bedroom below. Label all the things you're thankful for. Write, "Thank You God for..." at the top.

FridAy
//WANTS & NEEDS//

God uses people to do His good work. What do you want God to use you to do?

Fill in the blank: God, use me to _____.

You might pray, "God, use me to teach my friends about You." Or "God, use me to help people who need help." Or " God, use me to love others." *Think of ways you'd like to serve God.*

God, use me to _____

_____.

God, use me to _____

_____.

God, use me to _____

_____.

God, use me to _____

_____.

Saturday

//INTERCESSION//

Jesus tells us we should pray for our enemies. Who are your enemies? Who are the people who mistreat you? Who are you afraid of? Write their names and pray for them. You might draw a picture of one or two of them here. Maybe the picture will remind you that they're just humans, and all humans (even the mean and scary ones) need God's love.

WEEK 7

Monday
//THE LORD'S PRAYER//

When we pray "Your kingdom come, Your will be done on earth as it is Heaven," we're asking God to make things better.
What needs to be better? Make a list of things you want God to fix or improve and then ask Him to fix or improve them:

1.

2.

3.

4.

5.

Tuesday
//PRAISE//

Make a word map explaining what God is like. We've put God in the middle circle. Put words that describe God coming out from the center circle. Add as many circles as you'd like.

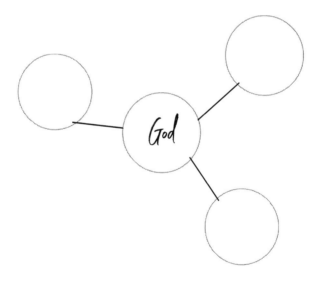

Wednesday
//CONNECTION//

What are you wishing for right now? Tell God about it. Tell Him what you think your life would be like if your wish came true.

Thursday
//THANKSGIVING//

Thank God for 4 things you don't like but you know are good for you:

1.

2.

3.

4.

Friday
//WANTS & NEEDS//

"Wise" means "able to make good choices" or "understand-ing." Do you want to be wise? Ask God to make you wise.

Do you have any choices you have to make?
What don't you understand?

Tell God about it, and ask for wisdom.

Saturday
//INTERCESSION//

Do you think you might get married someday? If so, pray right now for the person you'll marry in the future. What kind of a person do you hope they'll be? Ask God to help them become a good person who loves God.

WEEK 8

Monday
//THE LORD'S PRAYER//

Have you memorized The Lord's Prayer yet? Say it out loud ten times. Don't forget to pay attention to what the words mean.

Our Father Who is in Heaven,
Hallowed be Your name.
Your kingdom come, Your will be done
On earth as it is in Heaven.
Give us this day our daily bread
And forgive us our sins
as we forgive those who sin against us.
Lead us not into temptation
but deliver us from the evil one.

Tuesday
//PRAISE//

Search on your computer for "amazing animals" or "natural wonders." Take a few minutes to look at God's creation. Every time you see something amazing say, "God, You make amazing things."

Make a list of the amazing things you saw here:

Wednesday
//CONNECTION//

Tell God about your favorite TV show, book or video game. Tell Him why you like it so much. Give four reasons:

God, my favorite _____ is _____.

I like it so much because:

1.

2.

3.

4.

Thursday
//THANKSGIVING//

What's good in your friends' lives right now? Thank God for the good gifts He's giving your friends. List five good things that have happened to any of your friends:

1.

2.

3.

4.

5.

Friday
//WANTS & NEEDS//

Today let's pray this easy-to-read version of a prayer from St. Francis of Assissi. In it we ask God to make us the people He most wants us to be.

Lord, make me a person who makes peace.
When people show hate, let me show love;
when people hurt me, let me forgive;
when I feel doubt, grow my faith;
when I feel like giving up, give me hope;
when I find dark places, give me light;
when I'm sad, give me joy.

Master, help me not to care so much about myself but to care about others.

Saturday
//INTERCESSION//

God says it's our job to care for orphans and widows. Orphans and widows are people who don't have physical families. Orphans don't have parents, and widows are women whose husbands have died.

Do you know any orphans or widows? Do you know anyone who feels lonely or unloved? Pray for them. What do you want God to do for them? How do you want Him to make them feel?

WEEK 9

Monday
//THE LORD'S PRAYER//

In The Lord's Prayer, when we pray, "Give us this day our daily bread," we're asking God to give us what we need *today*. Think about today. What feels heavy? What seems too hard? Ask God to give you what you need so you can do what you have to do.

Tuesday
//PRAISE//

Go somewhere you've never prayed before. You might go outside and lie down on your back in the grass. You might climb a tree.

Now look around. Do you see God? Tell Him how awesome He is. Tell Him what He's like and what He's done.

Wednesday
//CONNECTION//

Do you have a secret? Tell God. (He already knows but He'd love it if you'd share it with Him.)

Thursday
//THANKSGIVING//

Thank God for the people in your life who take care of you. Write their names below and make a list of three things you like about each one.

Friday
//WANTS & NEEDS//

We don't always know what's best for us, but God does. Today let's take our prayer from the Bible. We'll ask God to help us do what He says He wants us to do.

Philippians 2:3-4 says, "When you do things, do not let selfishness or pride be your guide. Be humble and give more honor to others than to yourselves. Do not be interested only in your own life, but be interested in the lives of others."

Let's turn this verse into our prayer. Read this to God:

God, when we do things, help us not let pride or selfishness be our guide. Make us humble. Help us give honor to others. Help us be interested in other people's lives and not just our own.

Saturday
//INTERCESSION//

Do you have a favorite sports team, favorite singer or favorite actress? Pray for the team's players (or the singer or actress) by name. Don't pray that they'd do well in their work, pray that they'd come to know God better. Pray that God would lead them and love them and bless them.

WEEK 10

Monday
//THE LORD'S PRAYER//

Use The Lord's Prayer as a skeleton for your conversation with God (again). Add your own words and needs to The Lord's Prayer below:

Our father who is in Heaven, hallowed be Your name.

Your kingdom come, Your will be done, on earth as it is in Heaven.

Give us this day our daily bread.

Forgive us our sins as we forgive those who sin against us.

Lead us not into temptation but deliver us from the evil one.

Tuesday
//PRAISE//

Make Psalm 23:1-4 your own by filling in the blanks with words that make sense:

The Lord is my _____. I have everything I need.

He gives me _____.

He leads me to _____.

He gives me new _____.

For the good of his name, He leads me on paths that are _____

_____.

Even if I _____, I will not be afraid because You are with me.

Wednesday
//CONNECTION//

Tell God about something that made you really, really happy.
Write or draw about it.

Thursday
//THANKSGIVING//

Some days it's easy to think of things to thank God for. Some days it's hard. Don't worry. God wants to hear about what's good AND what's bad. Make two lists:

God, Here's What's Bad	God, Here's What's Great

Friday
//WANTS & NEEDS//

What are you good at? Make a list of your talents. Don't be shy. God made you good at lots of things! Ask God to help you use those talents for Him.

God, You made me. Here are the things You know I'm good at doing:

Help me use these talents for Your glory.

Saturday
//INTERCESSION//

Pray for the leaders at your church by name. You can probably find a list of their names on your church's website.

Pray for elders, deacons, ministers and women's and children's ministry leaders. If you don't know what that means, ask your parents for help making your list.

Ask God to give these people wisdom, passion, courage, joy, perseverence... Anything you think they need to do their work for God.

WEEK 11

Monday
//THE LORD'S PRAYER//

Today, ask God not to lead you into temptation but to deliver you from the evil one. Basically you want to ask God for protection from the devil (the devil only always wants you to do bad things). What bad things has the devil been encouraging you to do lately? Write them down. Then, ask God to make the devil shut up.

Tuesday
//PRAISE//

Let's do another praise simile--that's what it's called when we say, "God, You are like a _____.

Compare God to two things. Explain how He's like those things.

God, You are like a _____.

Because You_____

_____

God, You are like a _____.

Because You_____

_____

God, You are like a _____.

Because You_____

_____

Wednesday
//CONNECTION//

What do you think it's like to be God? Fill in the blanks below:

God, it must be cool to be You when _____

_____

_____

_____

_____

_____

God, it must be hard to be You when _____

_____

_____

_____

_____

_____

_____

Thursday
//THANKSGIVING//

Who are your three best friends? Write their names and list two reasons per friend why you're thankful to God for their friendship.

Thank You, God, for friends!

Friday
//WANTS & NEEDS//

Ask God to help you follow these Proverbs. Draw yourself doing the right thing...

"The honest person will live safely. But the one who is dishonest will be caught." (Proverbs 10:9)

"Hatred stirs up trouble. But love forgives all wrongs." (Proverbs 10:12)

Saturday
//INTERCESSION//

Today let's pray for peace. Where in the world are people at war? Make a list of countries. You might ask your parents for help or look it up on the Internet. Pray for each country on your list. Ask God to help them stop fighting.

WEEK 12

Monday
//THE LORD'S PRAYER//

When we pray and ask God to "Forgive us our sins as we forgive those who sin against us," we're asking God to forgive us just as much as we forgive other people. Are you good at forgiving other people? Has anyone hurt your feelings? Who do you need to forgive?

List people you need to forgive here. Ask God to help you forgive.

Tuesday
//PRAISE//

Let's praise God today in song. Did you know songs could be prayers? What's your favorite song to sing to God? Climb inside your closet or go outside to sing it. Make sure it's a song that tells God how great He is. Sing it really, really loud with your whole heart. Write your favorite words from the song here:

Wednesday
//CONNECTION//

Do you ever worry about the future? About getting older? Tell God what you worry about. Tell Him what you're afraid might happen or what you're worried won't ever happen.

Thursday
//THANKSGIVING//

Every human needs a few basic things: Food, water, shelter, clothing. Do you have those things? Thank God for them.

Walk around your house or apartment thanking God for what you see.

Look through your closet. Thank God for the clothes and shoes you see.

Turn on the faucet in your bathroom sink and thank God for clean water.

Open your refrigerator or pantry. Thank God for the foods you find there.

Friday
//WANTS & NEEDS//

What are you bad at? Make a list of three things:

1.

2.

3.

Ask God to either make you better OR to help you give yourself grace. Sometimes it's perfectly okay to be bad at something. :)

Saturday
//INTERCESSION//

Today, pray with and for someone. Out loud. Find someone who would like to be prayed for. Maybe a relative or a friend at school or someone at church. Put your hand on their back or shoulder and pray asking God to help and bless them.

Who did you pray for?

WEEK 13

Monday
//THE LORD'S PRAYER//

Pray The Lord's Prayer. What part of this prayer do you need to pray the most today?

Our Father Who is in Heaven,
Hallowed (Special) be Your name.
Your kingdom come, Your will be done
On earth as it is in Heaven.
Give us this day our daily bread
And forgive us our sins
as we forgive those who sin against us.
Lead us not into temptation
but deliver us from the evil one.

Tuesday
//PRAISE//

Draw a picture of God. Be sure to label it. When you're done, describe it to God.

Wednesday
//CONNECTION//

In Psalm 6 David tells God exactly how he feels. He says, "I am tired of crying to You. Every night my bed is wet with tears. My bed is soaked from my crying. My eyes are weak from so much crying."

Now it's your turn. Tell God exactly how you're feeling right now. Are you happy? Sad? Excited? Nervous? Angry? Tell God all about it.

Thursday
//THANKSGIVING//

What are you feeling grateful for today? Name as many things as you can. Fill this page. Thank You, God, for...

Friday
//WANTS & NEEDS//

Think about yourself as an adult. What do you want to be like? What do you want to do for a job? For fun? Do you want a family? Draw a picture of the adult you'd like to be one day. Pray to God asking Him to help you become that person.

Saturday
//INTERCESSION//

Pray for someone who's much older than you are. Ask God for whatever you think he needs.

Pray for someone who's younger than you. Ask God for whatever you think she needs.

Pray for someone you think might be poor. Pray that God would provide for his needs.

Pray for someone you think might be rich. Pray that God would protect her heart.

Way to Go!

You finished your journal!!

You've been praying for 13 weeks. I bet you feel closer to God. I bet you feel stronger and better and happier. Doesn't that feel great?! Keep it up, friend!

Before you put this book away somewhere,
let me pray for you:

> Our Father in Heaven, be close to this child.
> Make her strong. Make him brave.
> Teach her to love. Teach him to be gentle and kind.
> Always meet her when she prays to You.
> Always listen when he shares his heart with You.
> We love You, God.
> In Jesus' powerful name we pray every day,
> Amen.

Made in the USA
Middletown, DE
18 March 2018